Crow Meadow
Meadow Crows

Drawings, Paintings, Poems by
Richard Metz

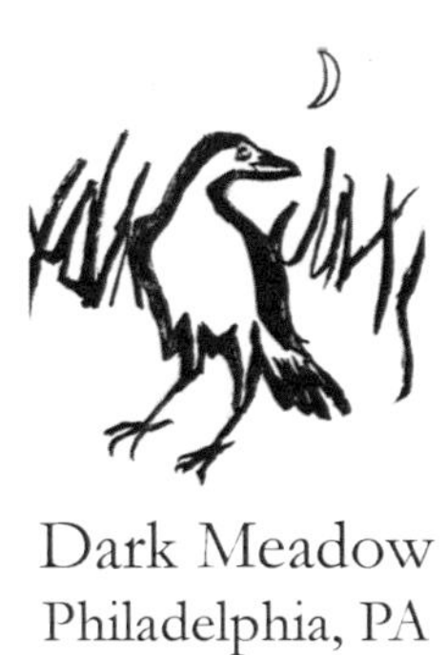

Dark Meadow
Philadelphia, PA

Published by Dark Meadow, 2026
Dark Meadow is an imprint of Frayed Edge Press

Cover image: Black Crow Flies
Back image: Calm Meadow

Library of Congress Control Number: 2025951304
ISBN: 9781642510737 (pbk.)
ISBN: 9781642510744 (Fireball pbk.)

Book production and layout by Parlew Associates, LLC

Publishers Cataloging in Publication

Names: Metz, Richard.
Title: Crow meadow : meadow crows / drawings, paintings, poems by Richard Metz.
Description: Philadelphia, PA : Dark Meadow, 2026.
Identifiers: LCCN 2025951304 | ISBN 9781642510737 (pbk.) | ISBN 9781642510744 (Fireball pbk.)
Subjects: LCSH: Crows – Poetry. | Ravens – Poetry. | Crows – Art. | Ravens – Art. | BISAC: POETRY / Subjects &
    Themes / Animals & Nature. | ART / Subjects & Themes / Plants & Animals. | NATURE / Animals / Birds.
Classification: LCC N7666.R38 M48 2026 | DDC 704.9432 M--dc23
LC record available at https://lccn.loc.gov/2025951304

Table of Contents

Introduction

Almost all of my work for the past four years is outdoor painting, in the meadows and woods of Southeastern Pennsylvania. Before painting, I just sit for a while, enjoying the breeze, the color, the movement, and the sounds and smells of the meadow. Perhaps I'm waiting for something. After a time, that something appears, and I begin a quick compositional drawing then on to painting. I use gouache because it is less hazardous, and allows for the kind of rhythmic brushstrokes that feel good, as well as being very easy to overpaint and adjust forms and color. I want to deepen my relationship with nature, and consider spending time there to be primary. Many places call me back over and over, and I record changes and creative observations of these meadows as spring becomes summer and fall, through painting and writing. My hope is that these works will inspire viewers to go further into nature and work for its protection and preservation.

I grew up near these areas and because I have a history, familiarity and knowledge of these places, it makes more sense to me to work in these Southeastern Pennsylvania meadows and woods. I consider that my study of these places expands me, and I hope that in some way these natural areas are getting to know me as well. This is not to negate the history of the lands, stolen from the Lenape Indians, worked as agriculture, sites of battles in the revolutionary war, part of landed estates and finally purchased by public entities for preservation. As a way of reciprocal thanks, I have worked for the last thirty-five years protecting natural areas.

Crows and ravens are serious birds, with loud harsh calls, and imposing black shapes, which contrast with the colors of the land. They are the most important birds in Native American cultures and written about extensively in Western culture from the Greeks to present day. I've had a simple relationship with the local murder of crows for ten years. Each morning, they come to the tall trees across the street and make a racket, knowing this is a signal for me to come out and feed them peanuts. This gives me a chance to study their movements, help them out a bit, and have a chance for a deeper relationship to grow.

My readings and observations of crows and ravens point to their intelligence, individuality, and their complex social relationships. I am convinced that crows and ravens have unique thoughts, make creative and calculated actions based on past experiences, and have a complex social bonding and hierarchies. Heinrich Bernd, the biologist and ornithologist who has written several books on crows and ravens, has concluded that to understand them, one must understand their relationship to their environment. My work seeks to portray that interconnectedness.

—Richard Metz
Philadelphia, 2026

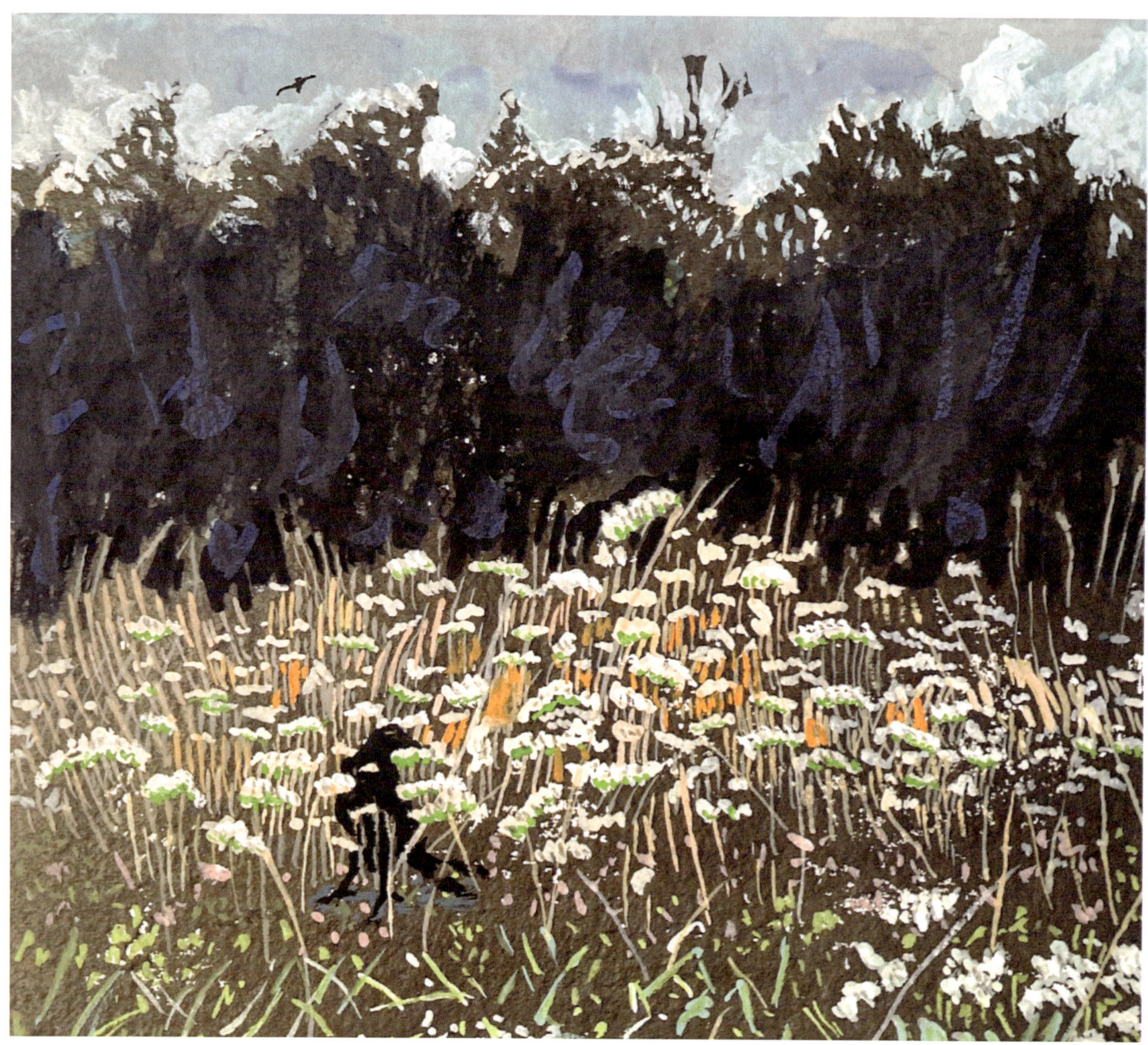

Dark Meadow

As the sun descends
at the end of the day,
I'm looking for worms
and edible creatures
to hold me over
through the long deep night

My friends are all leaving,
back to the roost,
settling in for the eve.
The shadows grow long
the trees in the distance
have become silhouettes

I made my case
to my erstwhile companions—
"The cool of dusk
allows for grace and reflection.
More critters come out
thinking darkness
protection."

Now softly I creep
under wispy tufts,
hiding and waiting,
blending in with the night.
They won't know I'm here
until it's much too late

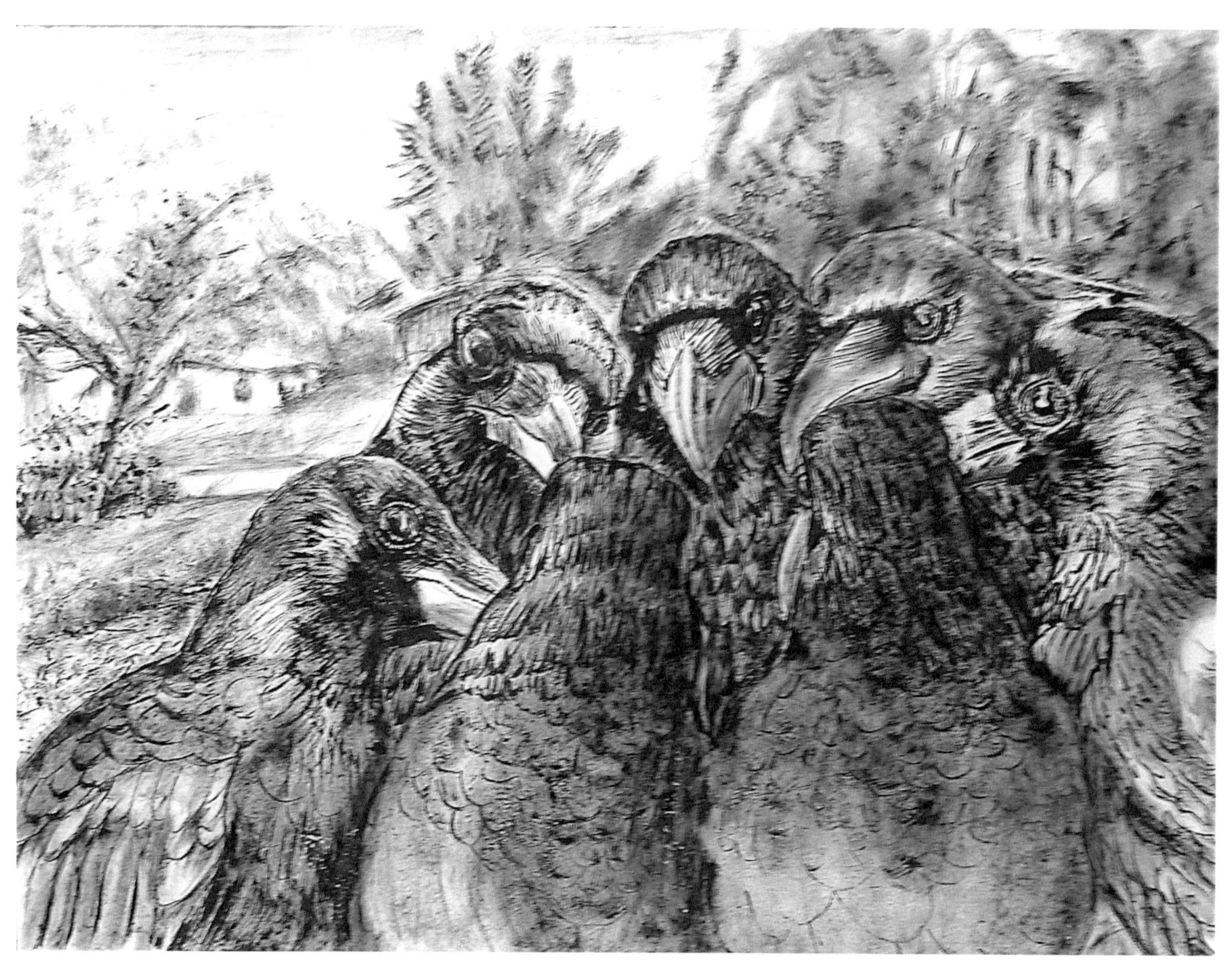

Grave Incident at the Morning Meeting

What've you done—befriending the hawk?
Where've you been—you're covered in ants?
What's that smell all about your wings?
The security of the murder invites close scrutiny
everyone is garbling—squawking in warbles
alive with love and concern.

Now-son of Xenth, tell us your travels:
"I glided down to a container of gold,
behind the place of cooked food
Began rooting and pawing, like mother had shown—
And—Yeeks! I jumped back—a whole human is in here—
Dead for a day, not more
streaks of blood covering his face, leaking from his leg

I've never encountered a human so close
splayed limbs, torn garments, a lifeless sad face
Then I remembered my great uncle Jxxcr—
'Humans are our a most ancient of meals.'
I took a small taste and twisted my mouth
then took another and more—

The next sunrise they came to bury their dead
They picked up his body and discussed his sad state
'Damn crows,' they uttered as they took him away."

———

The elders nodded and muttered,
glints and squints in their eyes—
"Nothing strange about that—
nothing strange, for sure."

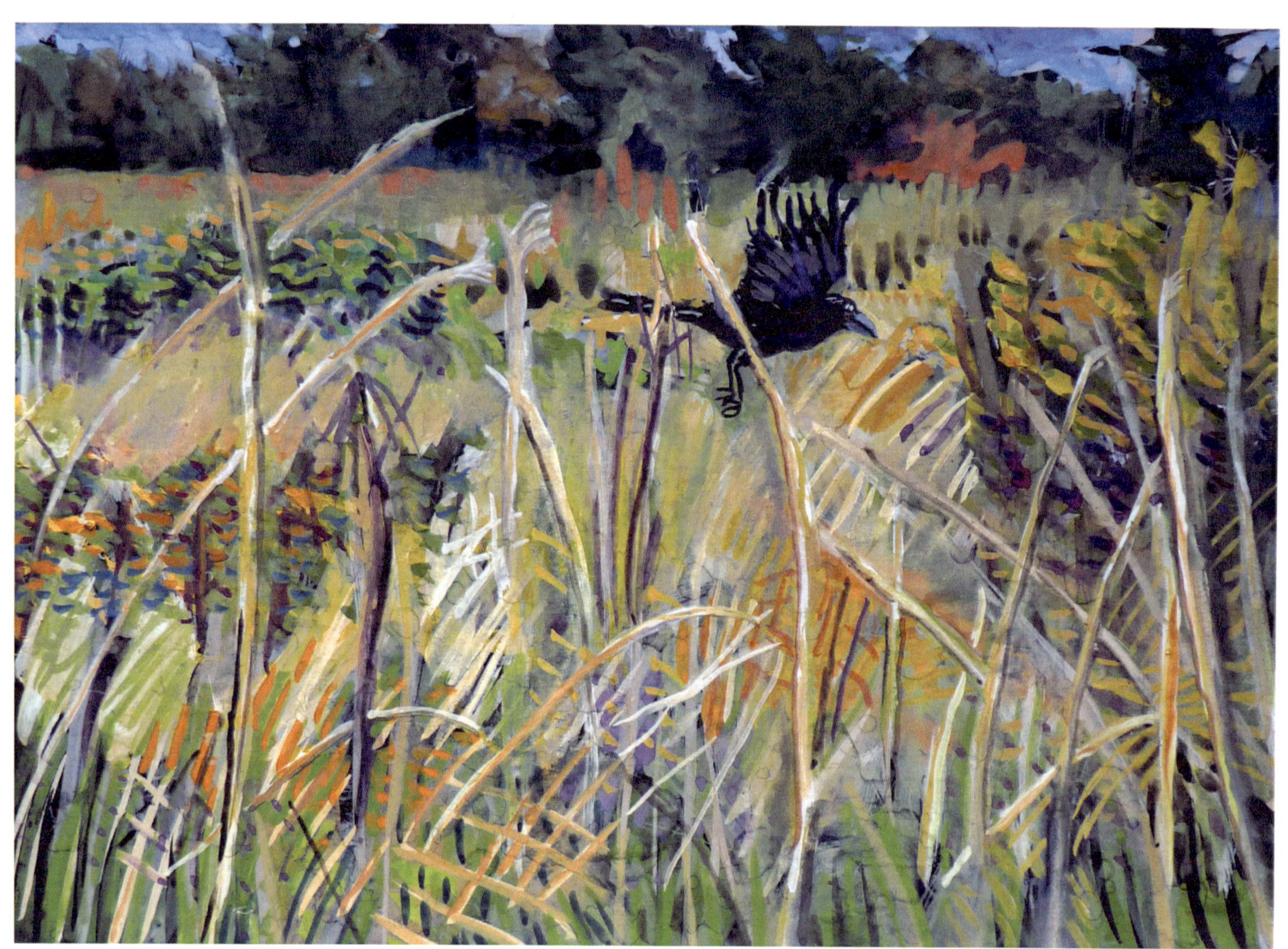

Long Meadow Low Flight

I'm flying low over blades of gold
that tickle my wings and tail
The purple soil is teeming with crawlers
waiting to gnash and fill me

The whooshing eddies and currents
winds whisper so loudly
There's a place for me here
between the meadow and sky

The weaving (of waving
sun-colored stalks in the distance)
speaks to me in glimmers
Deep below the summer yellow grasses,
little intricacies and mysterious spaces—
dark, waiting to be explored
Off in the distance, in another world
the verdant woods are humming

The price of flight is to live off the land,
to see the moving and edible—
to smell the dying, the rot
and the sweetness of berries and nectar
I can hear every creature's song
as the haloed late summer
draws me in

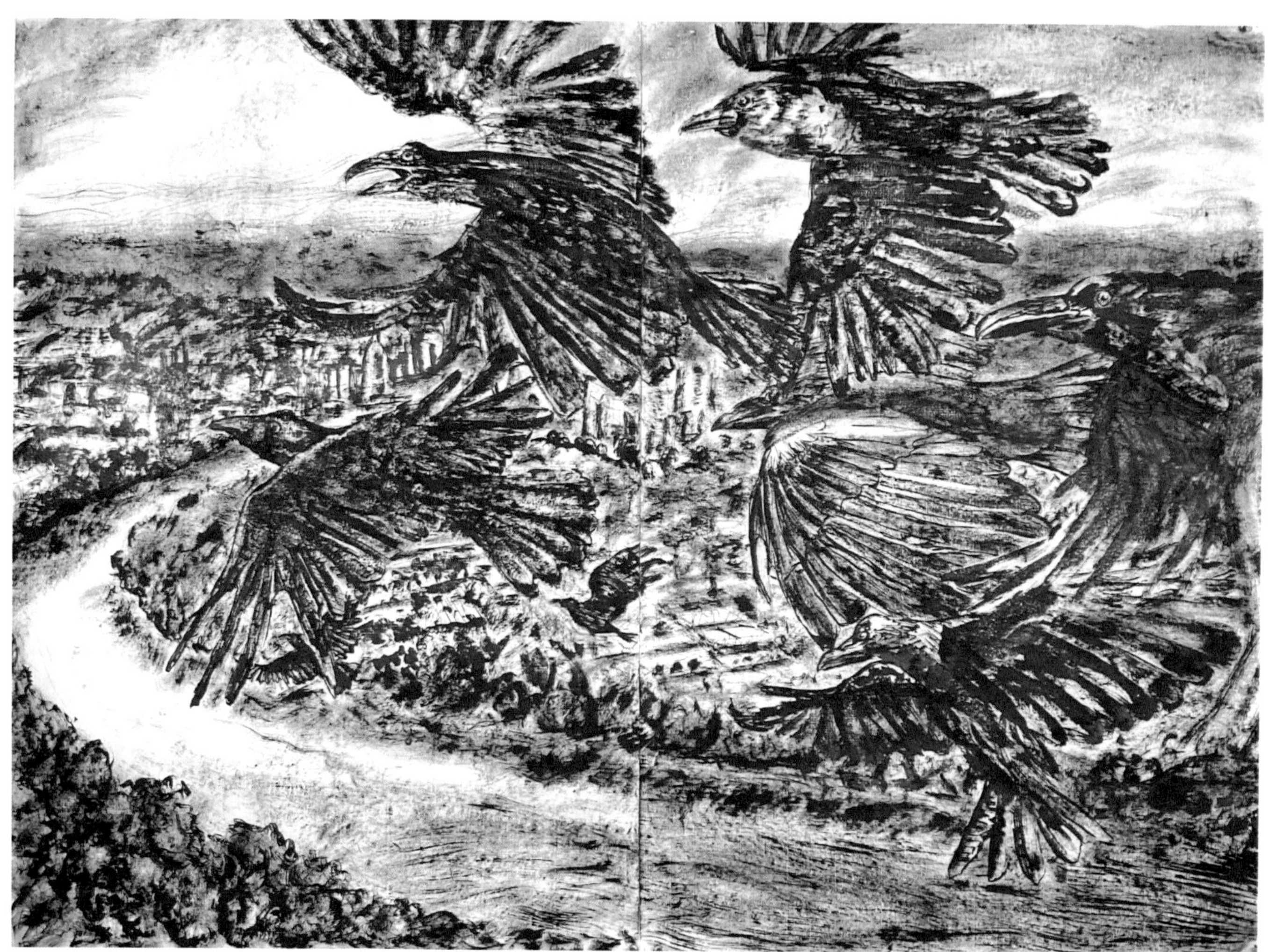

Bend in the River

Thundering music plays in our heads
in formation we ride the prevailing winds
up the river to the bend, miles from our roost

CaCaww Caw Caww, click click, cluck cluck

Smells of concrete, moldy plaster,
electricity, and smoke
a chemical that burns the nose
But ah once again,
the perfumes of frying and rotting

The strong rains are rushing the river
beware those mighty waters
Ocean salts in the wind from the east
clouds departing,
day on the rise

Prepare, my friends,
for some nasty local greeters
they'll be on us quick-as-a-blink
We must be cunning and tough
in a scrappy squabble

Then onto the town to
home in on the smells—
We'll have all day to find us a meal

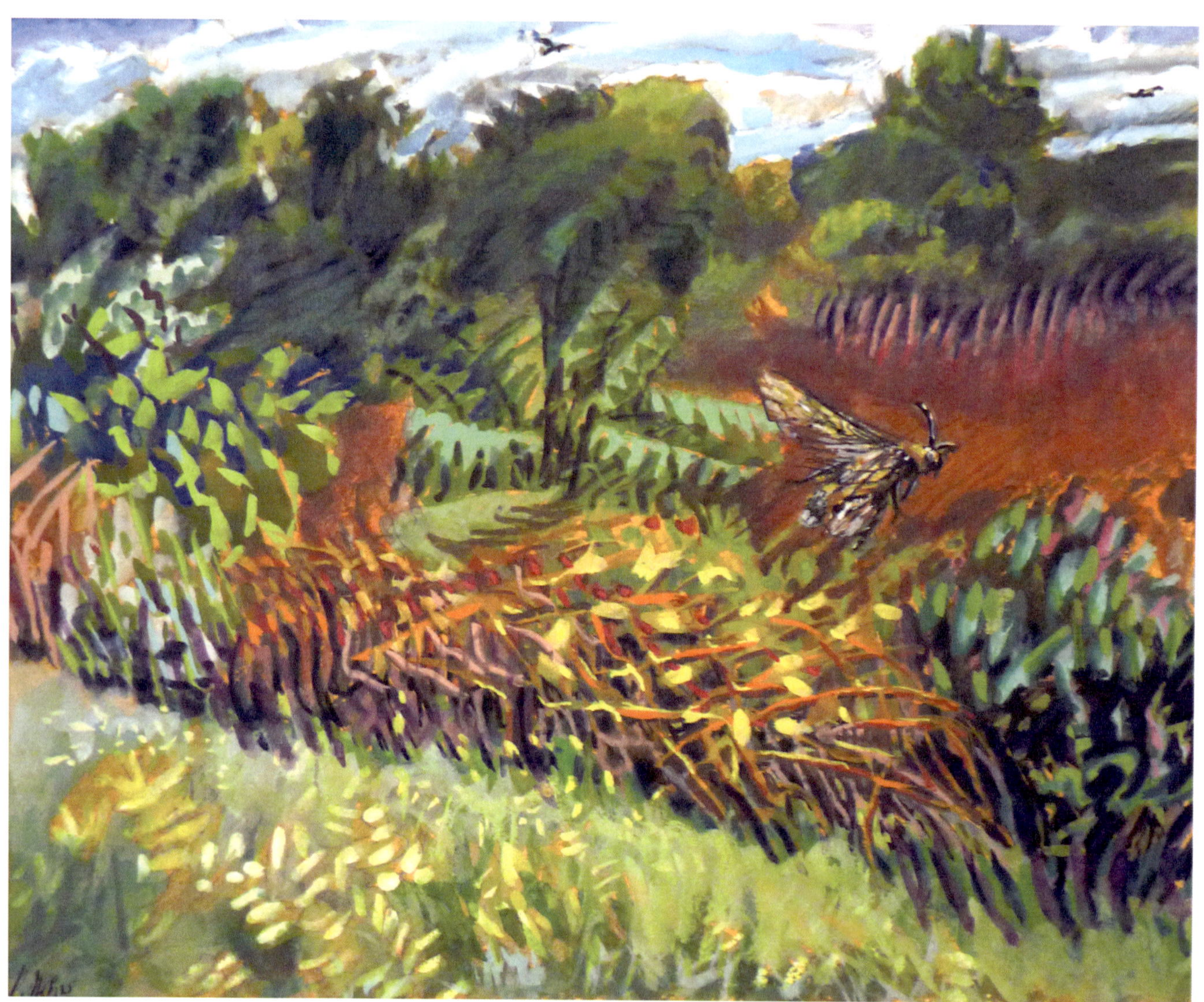

Red Love Bluebell

What would it mean if
you fell in love
with the deep buzzing meadow
down that dry dirt road?

Would you court her with flowers and chocolates?
Would you be jealous of the rascal Crows?
Would you send her cards with clovers and hearts
and dream about her at night?

Would you clean up your apartment
shower and shave, and dress
in your fanciest clothes,
wash your floors, scrub the stove, just in case
she decided to visit?

Would you say to her:
—I love the color of your soil—
and the curves of your hills?
Would you spend all day
walking round so slowly,
getting tangled in her vines,
getting high on her scent
brushing up against her grasses?

And surely you'll try to remember these days,
these eager early times
of a strange and tender love

And you're really quite certain
she returns your passion,
by the reds of her leaves,
the scent of her earth,
the serpentine dance she does
when the autumn wind blows

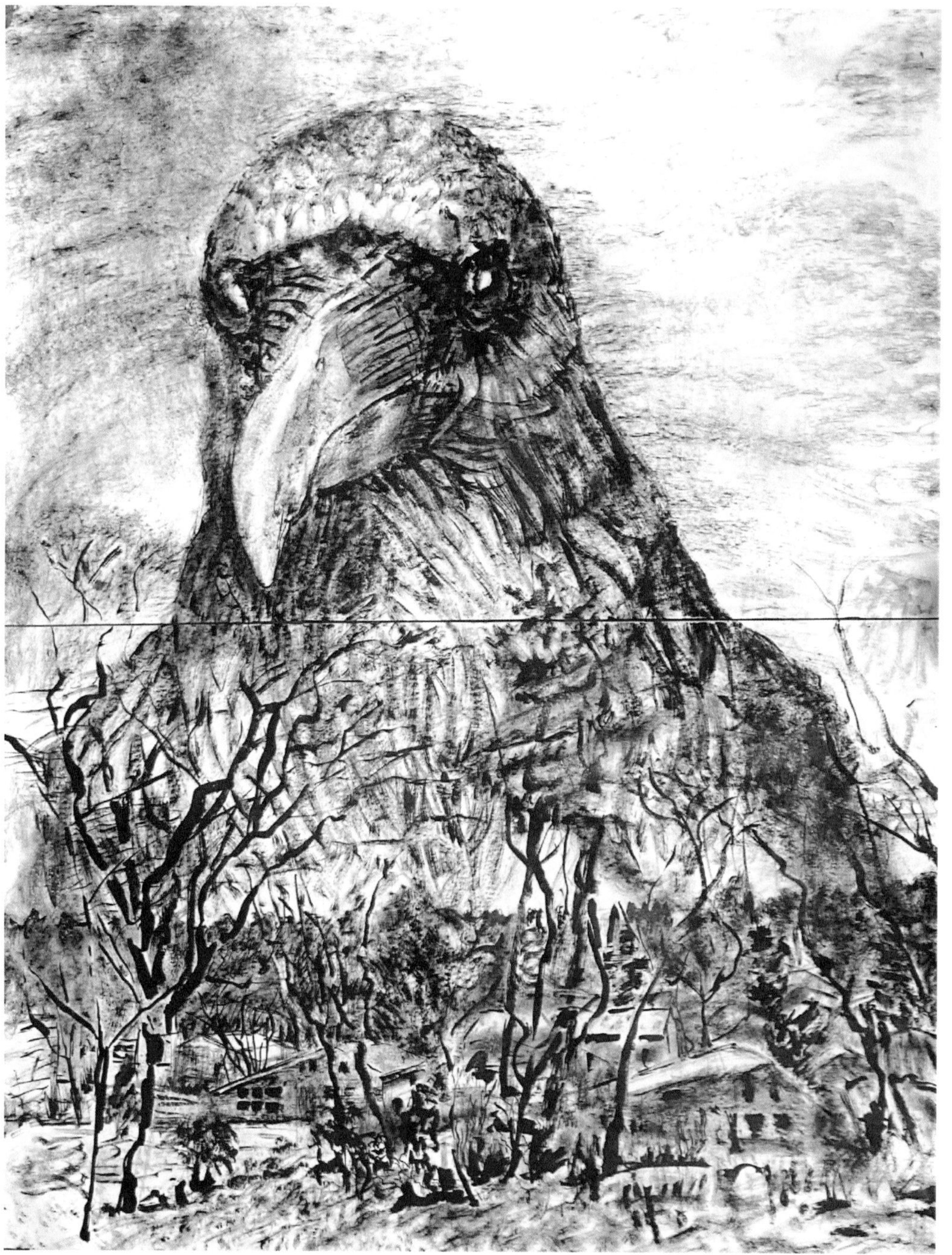

Occurrence Just Outside the City

It rose before dawn, waking us with a start
So tall, such eyes, such a threatening tone
We didn't appreciate it looming above
—a free people and all, we thought
Why was it here and what would it do?
How could you fight such a terrible fright?

It moves its head from side to side
What does it want when it raises its wings?
Some say it will eat us—they're quite upset
Look at that beak—it'll cut us to pieces
Some say it's here to protect us,
but how, and from what?
Some ask what we have done
to bring such a being upon us

Many shout, "It's evil," from their kitchen windows
The science crowd is fumbling and shrugging
"Not supposed to be. Illogical," they say

It lingers on into the afternoon sun
Stiff breezes push the trees back and forth
Then, just before four, it shook its head hard,
made such a sound we could no longer hear
ΛΛΛΛAAAWWWWWWWCC AAAAAAW
It's going to strike—Watch out

But no. It pauses. It must be a warning:
"Do what you must—don't wait until next we meet."
Around five it starts fading
and by six it was gone
but it's hours before we stop shaking

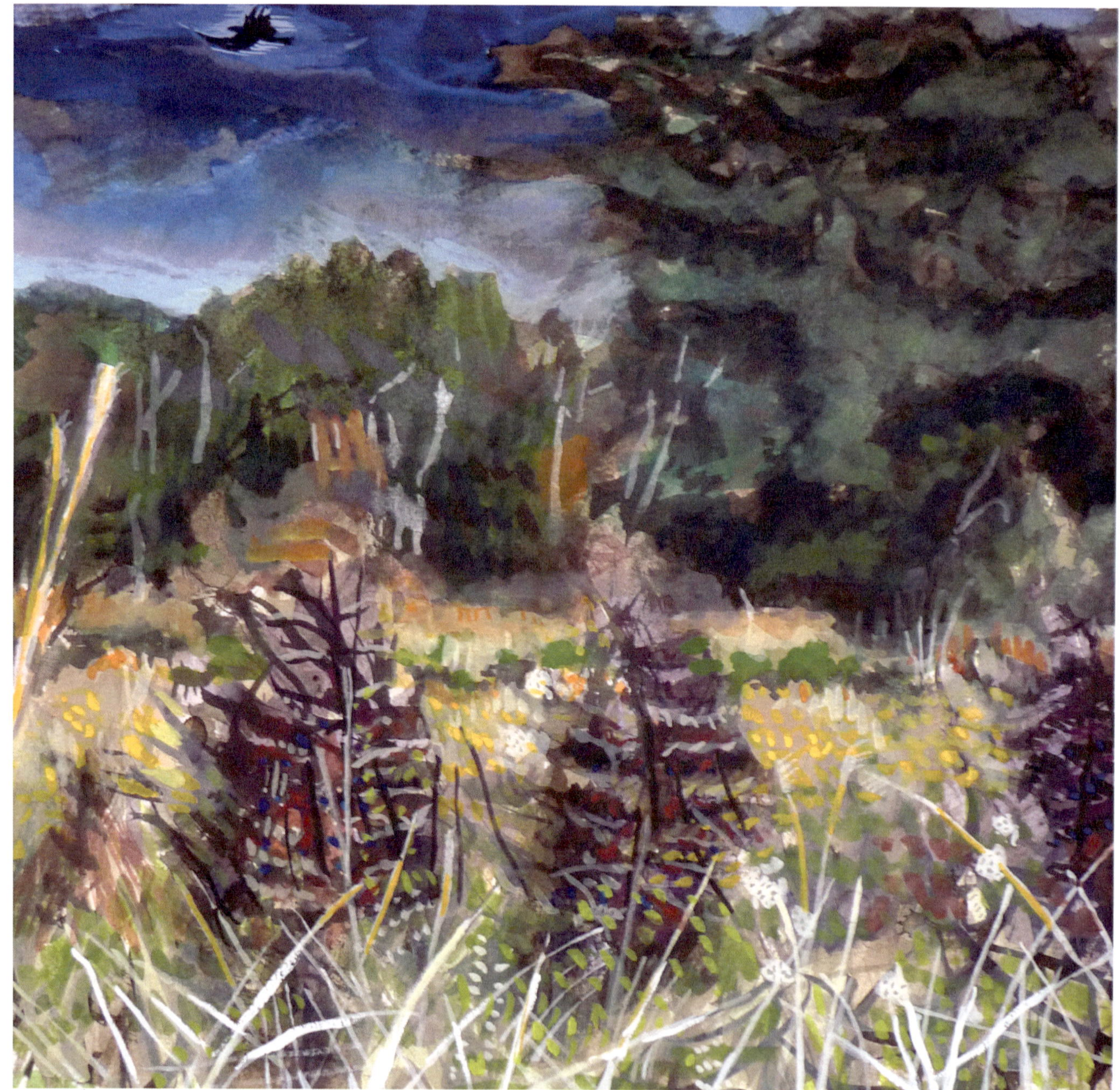

Strange Lands

Paused at the end of the world,
this comedy of terror and beauty
A wavering complexity—like galaxies
of seeds, grasses—stems, and leaves

Every plant nearby in bloom
faraway, faraway doom-doom
My brain has left but
I'm not bereft

For here we are, with johnny jumps
and soil lumps and corvid umps—
Such bouncing and darting
violent contrasts—charging violets
and bitter contentious yellows

An unmoored closeness to darkened skies
brings the late afternoon's conclusion—
We've never been here before—
Must we leave so soon?

Where is the last place you'd like
to visit before you close your eyes?

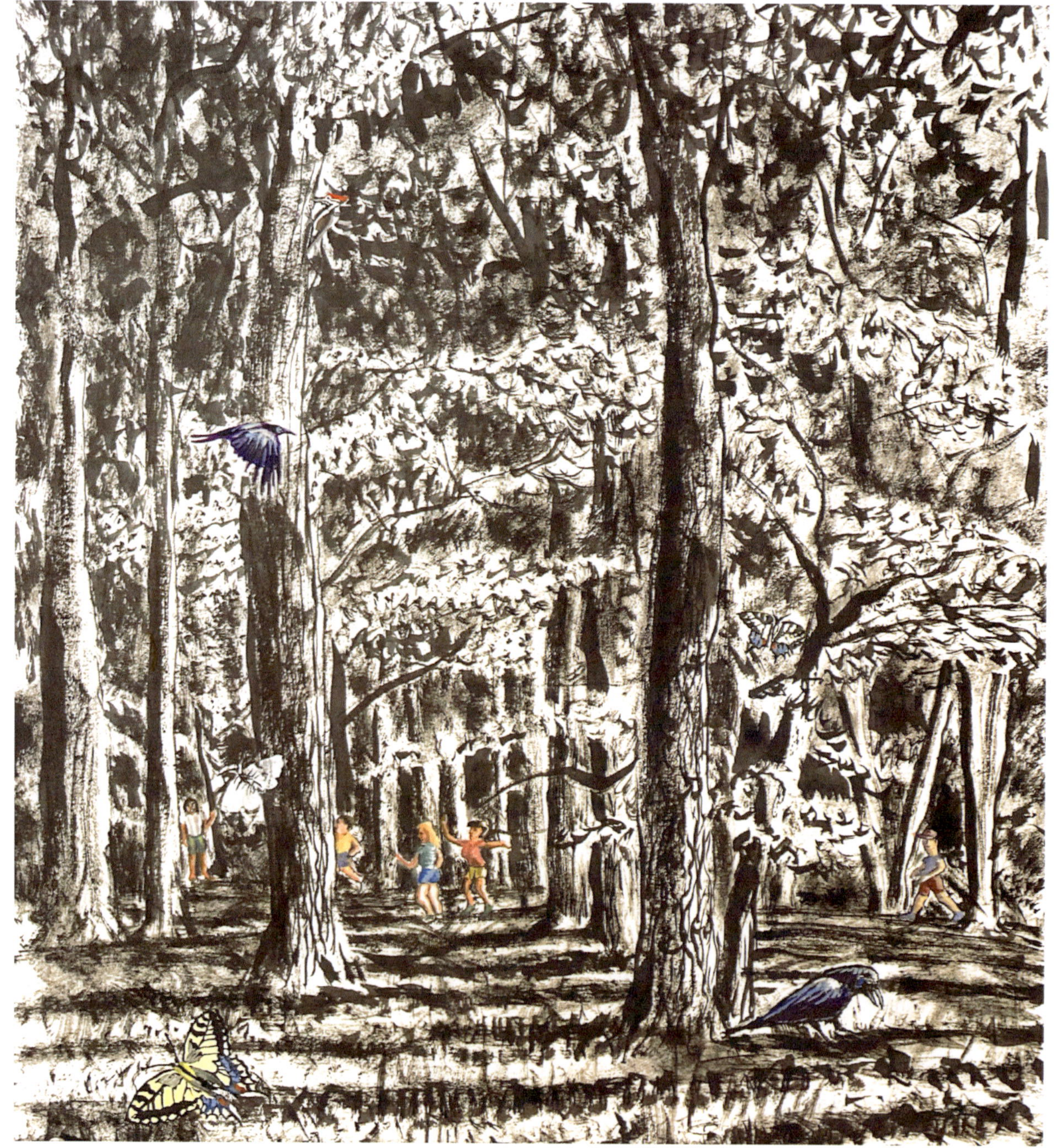

Risible Afternoon

What does it mean when suddenly
you can't hear a thing?
When a hush falls over the woods
and not even the wind is talking?
Why do you suddenly look peripherally
and get all jittery,
when the blurry edges are fixed
when your questions all scatter
across your own warm mind—
as the petals and leaves twinkle—
sliding down in the thick humid heat?

Turn your attention to a patchwork of patterns,
the details of browns and grays
on wiggly trees that stand far apart
Hold your breath as crows
scour the clearing for meals
Who's tapping along in the green shadows,
floating on the summer breath
grasping onto the mottled bark
red-head peeking and pecking so loud?

How entirely lovely this very fine day
for all of us beings in our wayside park—
Even the leaves laugh
in the butter blinding hot light—
laughing fluttering floaters
Let's all play in the sun—in the soft verdant spaces
under the bright speckled canopy of branches
In the indivisible, risible, invisible—insatiable,
uncontainable hereness and clearness of now

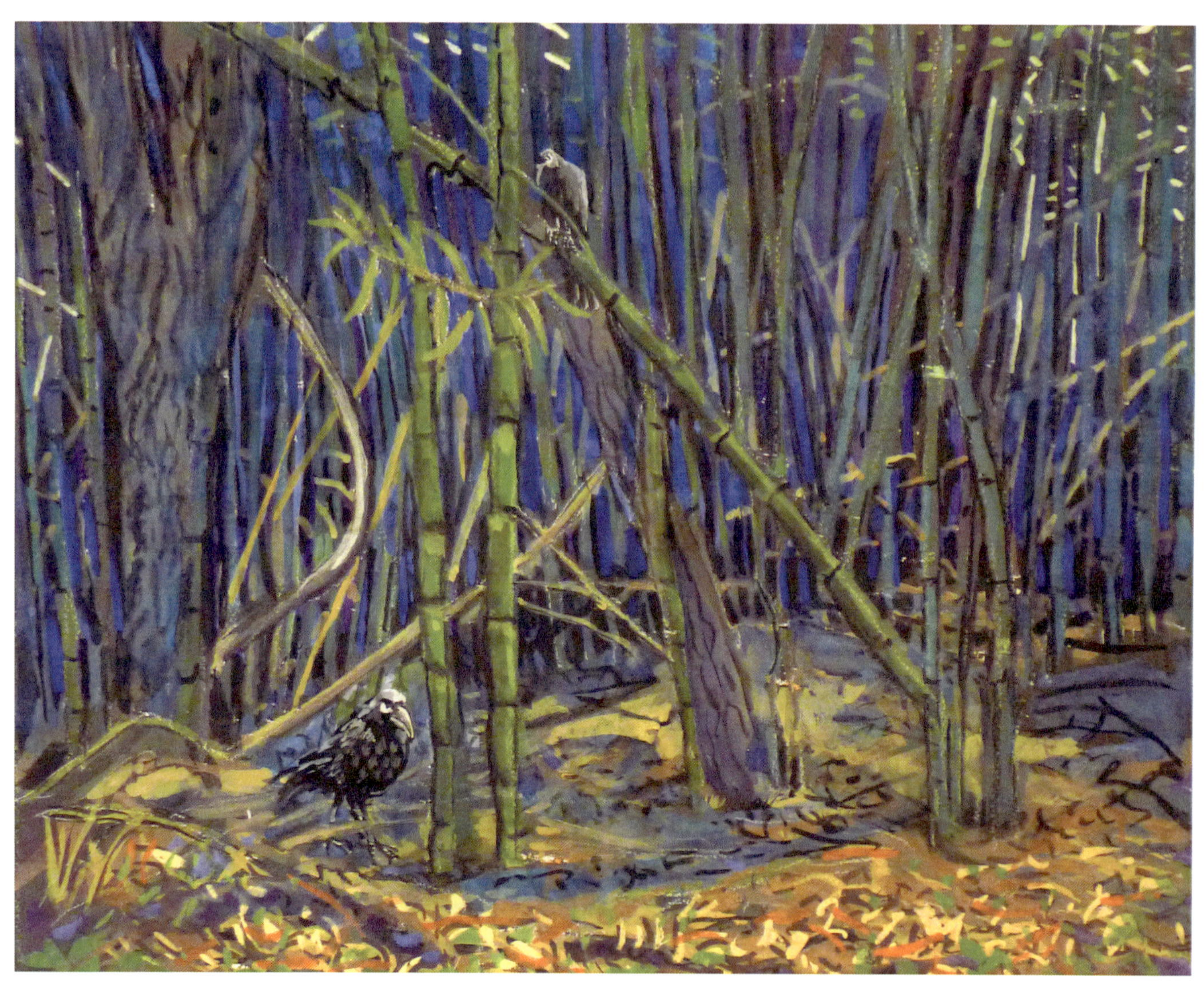

Bamboo Woods

Wandering, wondering
looking for the darkest place in the woods,
a place where it's night in the daytime

The bamboo woods stands tall and deep
cool in the heat of summer
oblivion's darkness the further we intrude
Cautioning—what's waiting for us inside?

Two crows—inky centurions—perched at the gate
investigating the shivering stalks
and the coming and goings inside
Our mind play tricks—the blackness is blue
or deepest shade of violet
Green stalks of bamboo
become a shining turquoise bath

Listen in—to the clicking and clacking
of a rhythm section drunk on the wind—
Mix the cymbals and brushes of the rustling leaves
with the knock knock of the bamboo high-hats—
drummers in the throes of the afternoon blues

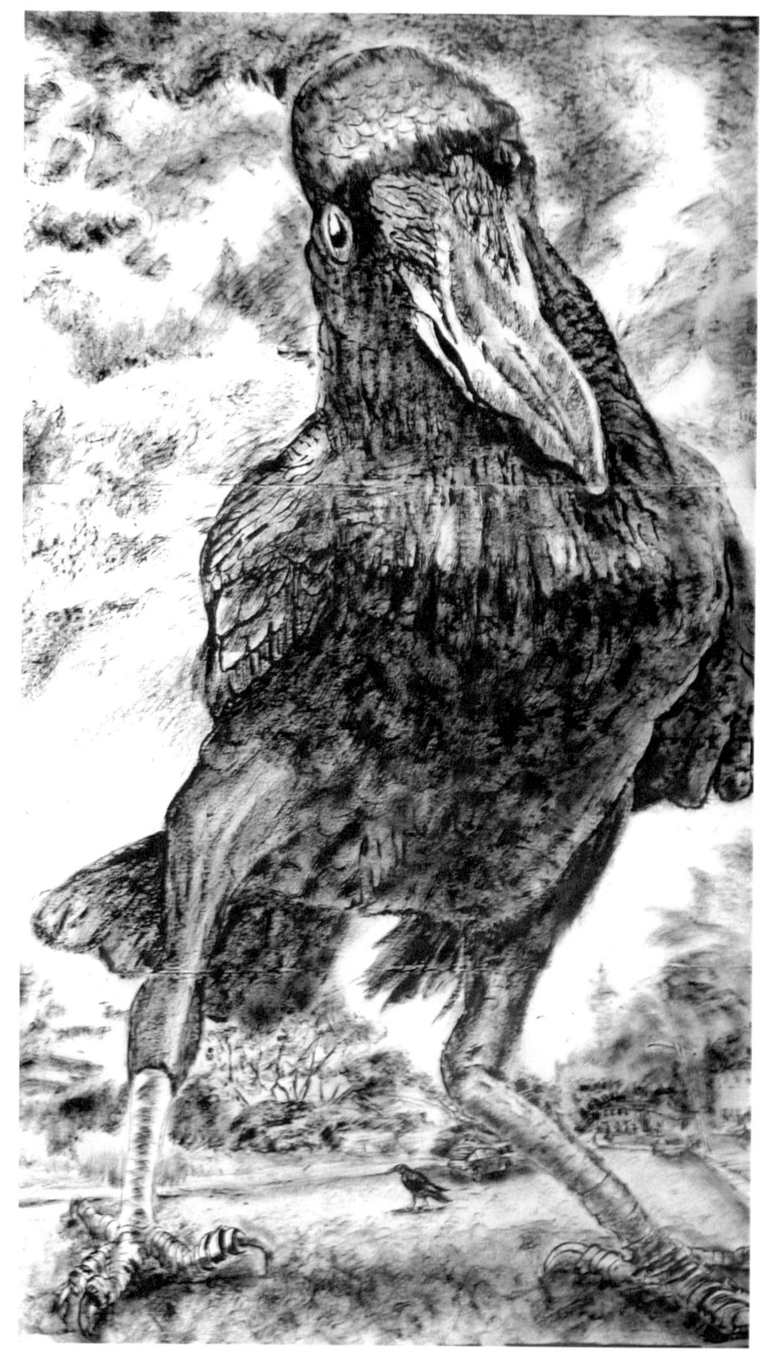

Wise Guy

You're talking to me like a friend,
not the enemy everyone says
Don't run away; don't be scared
I'll not attack you, my humanoid friend

Of course we're quite different—
you with big bones and skin,
me with feathers and claws
and hard-as-rock beak

Pshhhhaaaa, Cawwwwww,
We don't hafta be sworn one against one
Let's be civil, calm—even kind
For we've lived together for a thousand years
———
We'll push down the garrulous lanes
and circle 'round for a view
The glimmering crowd is abuzz
coming and going and sloshing about

We saunter so tall into the square
as the last long light is ebbing
Caw Caw Caw, the evening's festivities
have, at last, begun
"To the market," we cry, "for fishes and milk."
The labors the town will provide

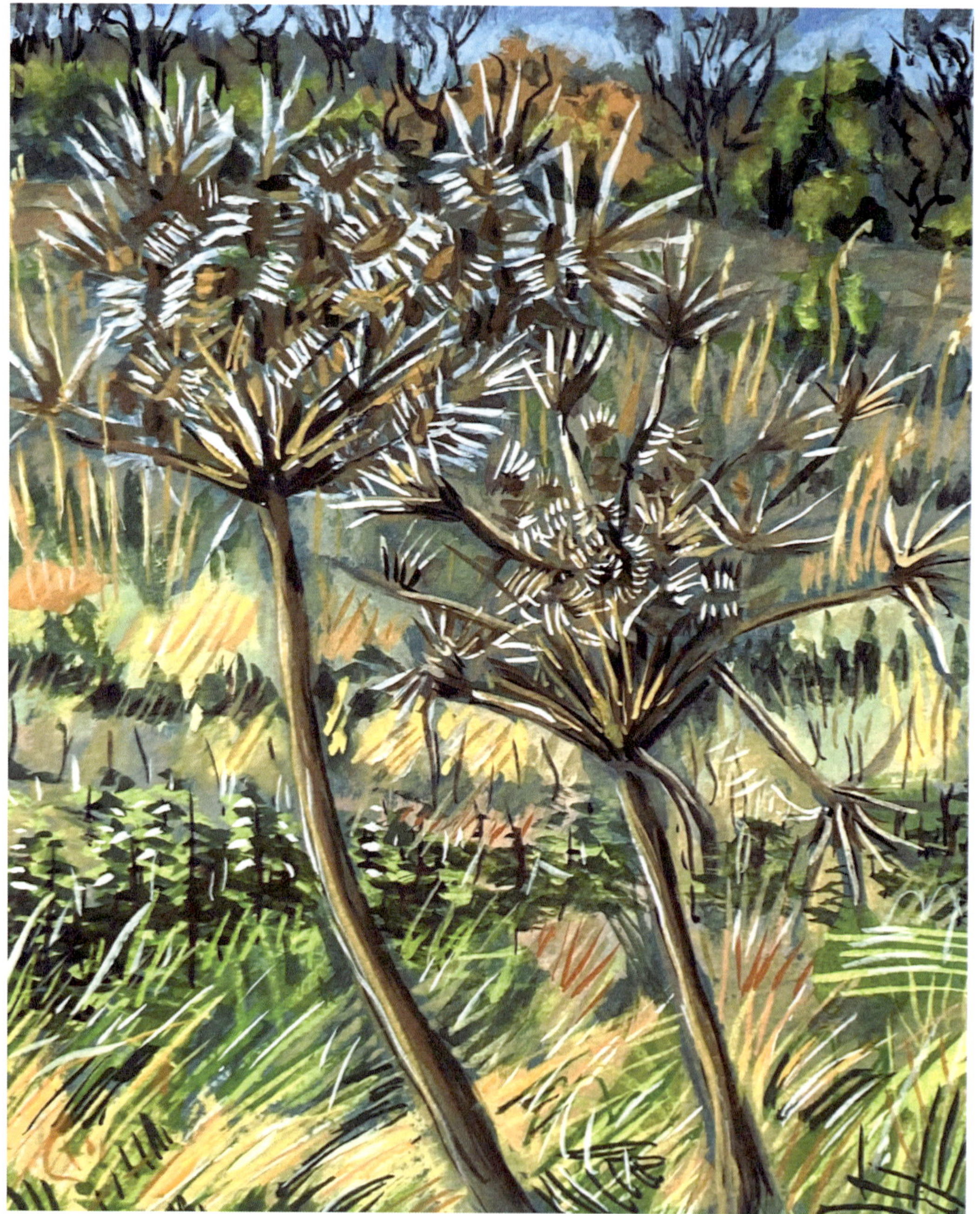

Queen Anne's Meadow

As the day wears on,
she lets her seeds fly
on the soft clear winds
of this blue afternoon

Like a universe of stars
shooting outward and free,
the seeds of Queen Anne
alight through the meadow

With a structure of cells,
molecules invisible,
stills of explosions and suns,
Queen Anne confirms what we
always suspected:

The structures of the world—
the moves, and designs
are consistently the same,
from atoms and sparks
to the grandest galaxies
of light

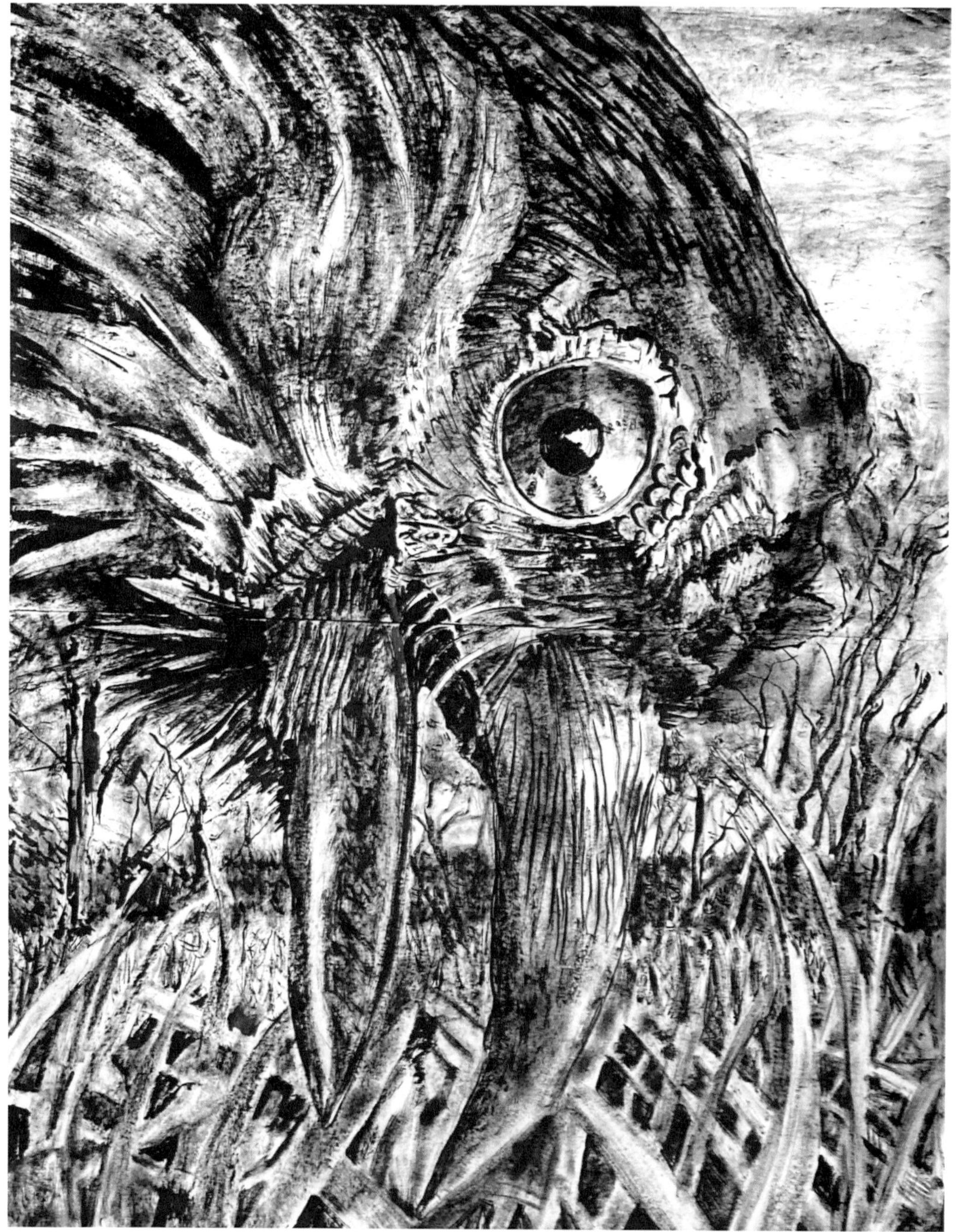

Up Close, in the Field

We are much too close,
never ever so close,
to this bipedal being.
Is he as nervous and wary as I?
Does he perceive me
as the threat?

Why is this human asleep,
curled in the grass—
like a cat or maybe a mouse?
His eyes aren't like mine,
nor his head or coat
My wings he won't have
or my sharpened clenched claws

The humans live in that structure of wood
and leave in the wheeled metal machine—
One's often outside, digging black loam,
when the trees and flowers
are in full bloom

Do they dream of family
and the dangers that prey?
Do their thoughts consider
the wonder of breathing,
and the speed of the air
in the boldest of May?

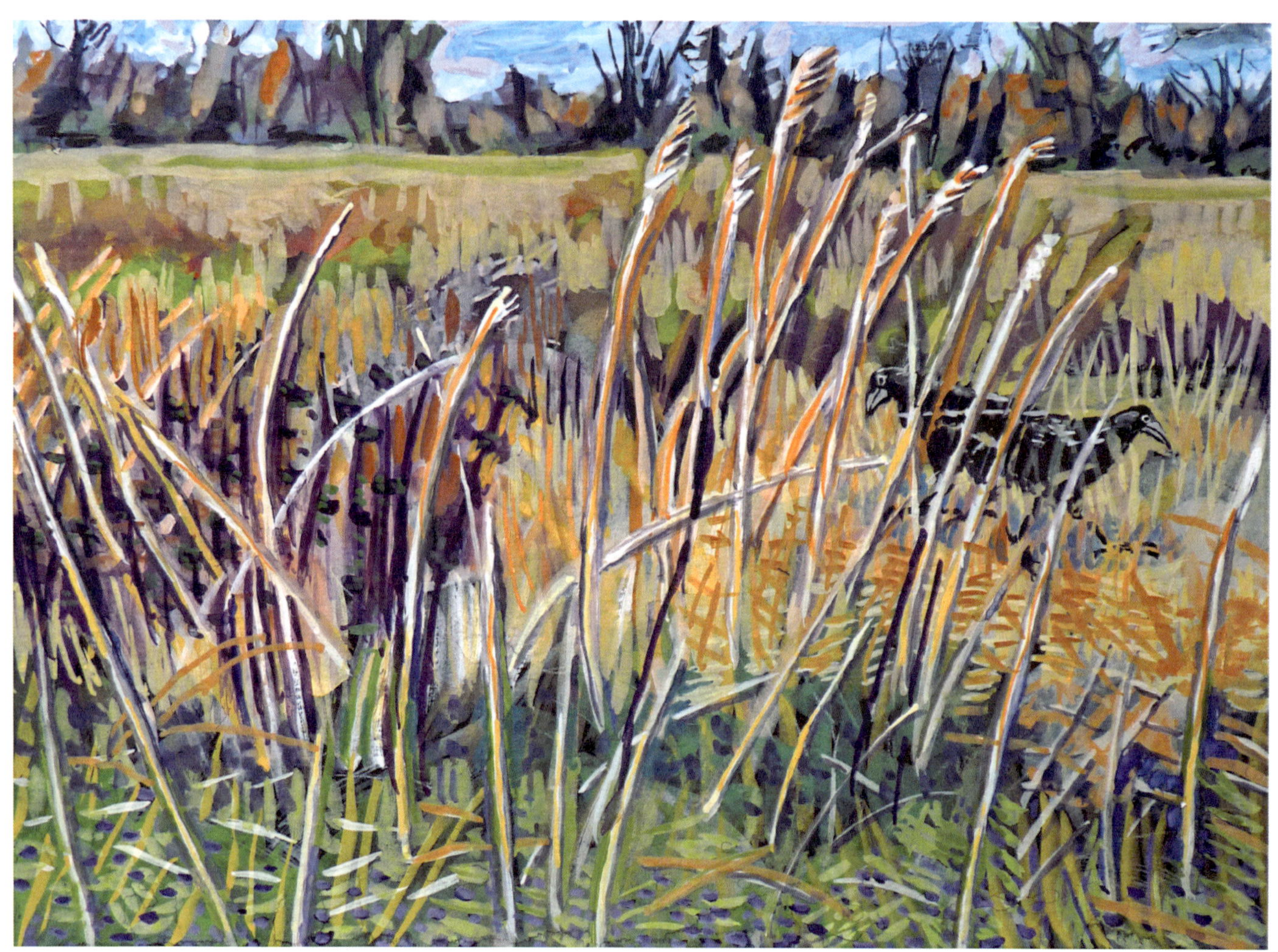

The Canary Sedge

Early on, a clarity in the air
Later—the over-baking summer

Cooler days are coming
I can smell them
But now when soil's still warm—
will the sun ever go down?

Still bounty enough
for all of us—
We pitch black birds,
are moving and hiding
in the drying
Canary Sedge

Trampling the sienna soil
pass through viridian grasses—
We are part of
all that surrounds—

We belong here now
not over there
in the pale distance
beyond the swaying trees

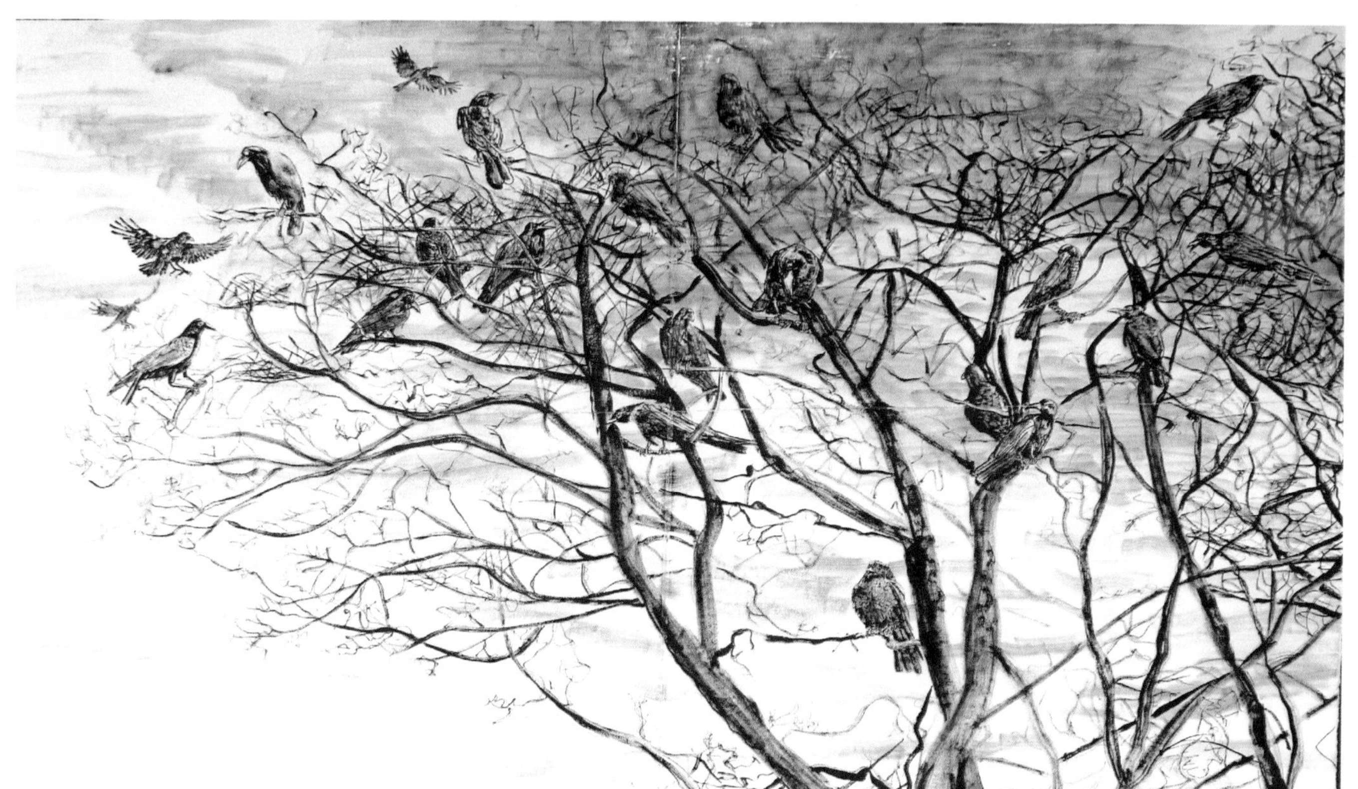

The Roost so Grand

Darkness is coming, the sky disappears
everyone's counting to make sure we're here,
Who's turn on lookout for owl and hawk?
"Where's your partner? Are they lost or…?"
"He'll be here, I'm sure—just taking his time."
"What happened to you? Was it a fight near the nest?"
"Your feathers are quite the mess."

Time to rest for us all, as a snowblur of sky settles in
Cool breezes—slightly moist, slightly sweet—
lighting upon our burnt-wood blackness

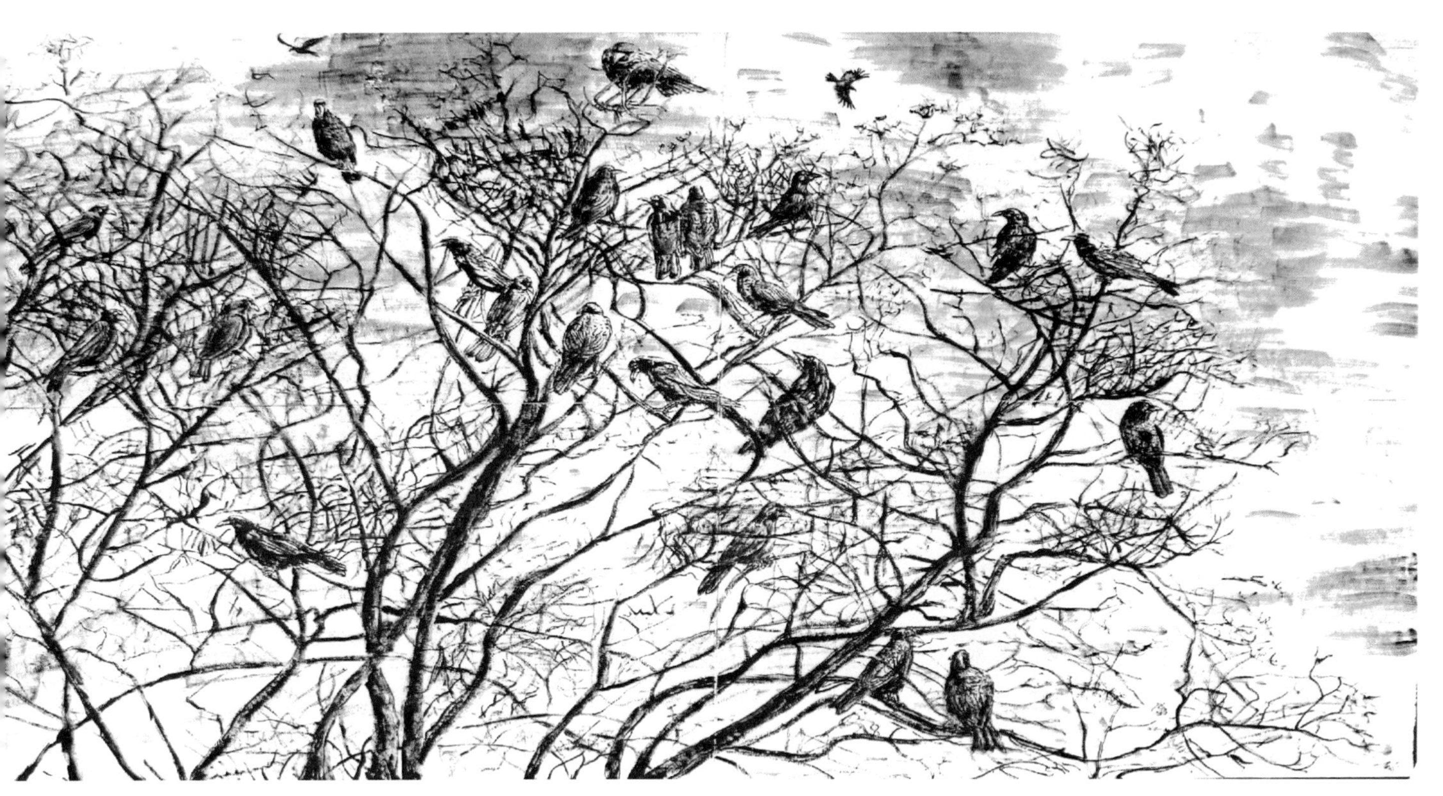

Waiting and watching—secure in our roost
Strength is in our assembly
Stillness an illusion the hours dispel

Passing the evening in quiet conversations:
places to eat, dangers to face,
the rabid, the foe, the wild, and feral
Those squirrels that climb all about our nests
will yet find a claw stuck deep in their back

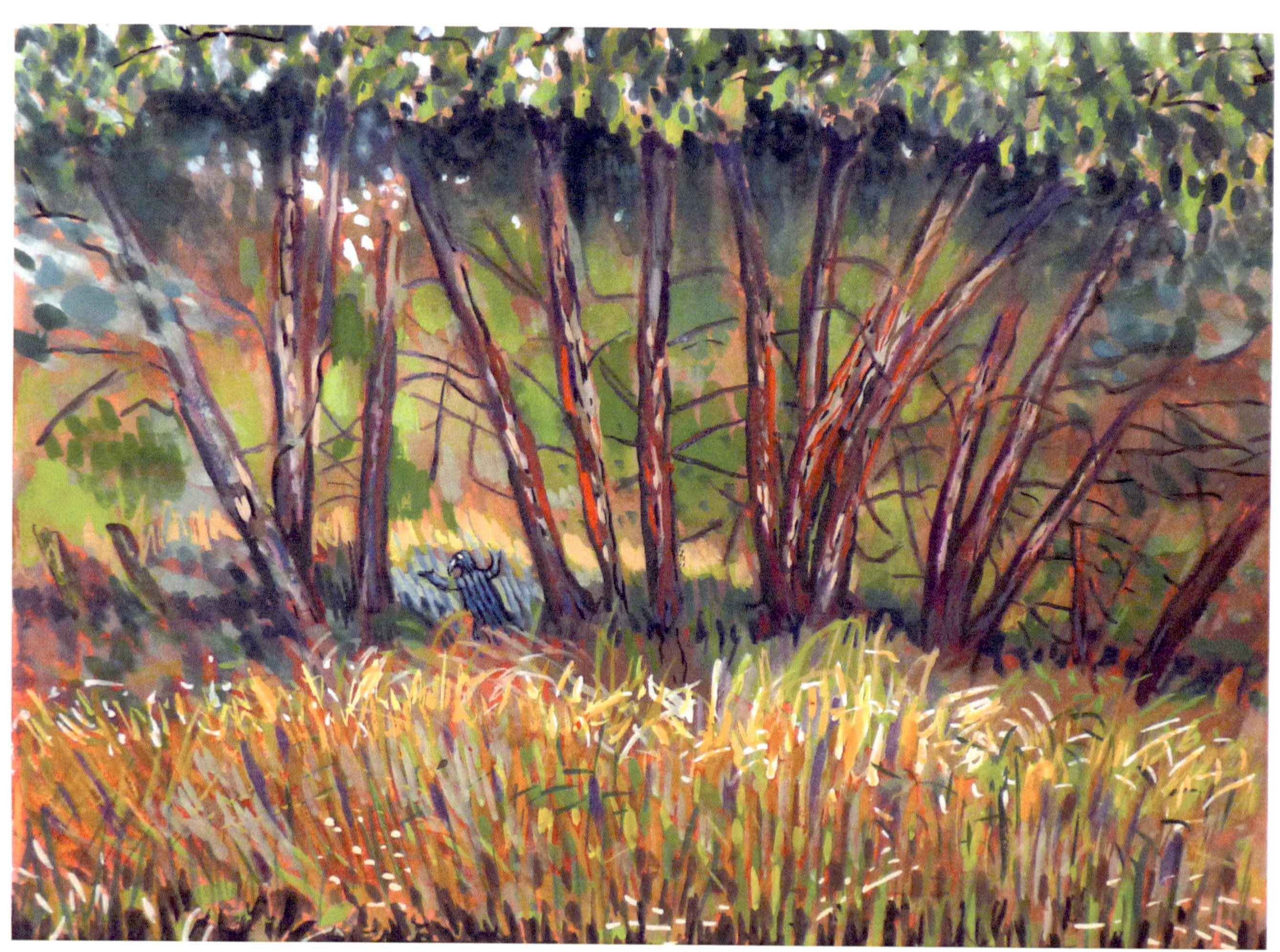

Red Trees

I saw myself running
    Blue and through
with bird beak and feathers—
    pursuing red trees
electric with light

Back of your throat red
    bloody hands red,
 long satisfying love red
    Red-through-green red

Sounds coming from my lips,
    like the swishing of leaves
 the wavering of crickets
    the hiccups of frogs and toads

Why are you running out there
    with rough abandon
barely a leg under you
    drunk with your visions?

Past a threshold yes—
    the refuge
to another world
    …where I belong

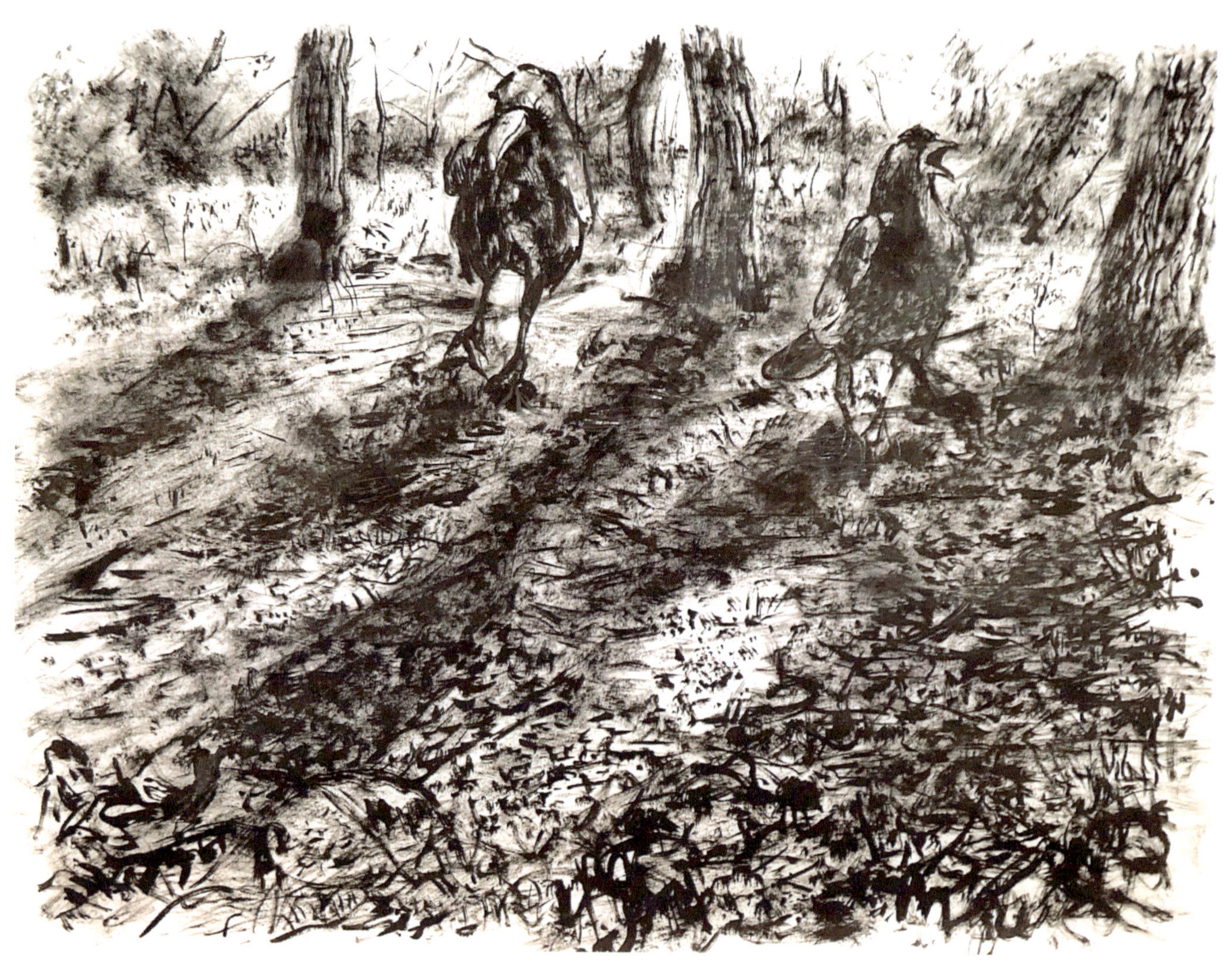

Argumentative Crows

Crackle Caw Caw
crunk crackle Caw Caw—
"I declare this space is ours,
this place, right now.
No one else must come near,
I declare, I declare"
"Must you, must you,
must you bellow and boast?
Such peace and quiet
and you fuss and shout about"

Leaves—very scurry,
Sticks—shaky shivey
and the tall brown grass
so woovey-woovey-woo
Everyone is jumping
when you look more closely—
And we do look very closely
for breaks in the patterns, for the recesses,
twinkles and squiggly things—
See here—there they are

And before the shadows overtake us
and the gold disappears from the sky,
Let's take one last stroll,
a final parade in the
whispering laughter of the fading day

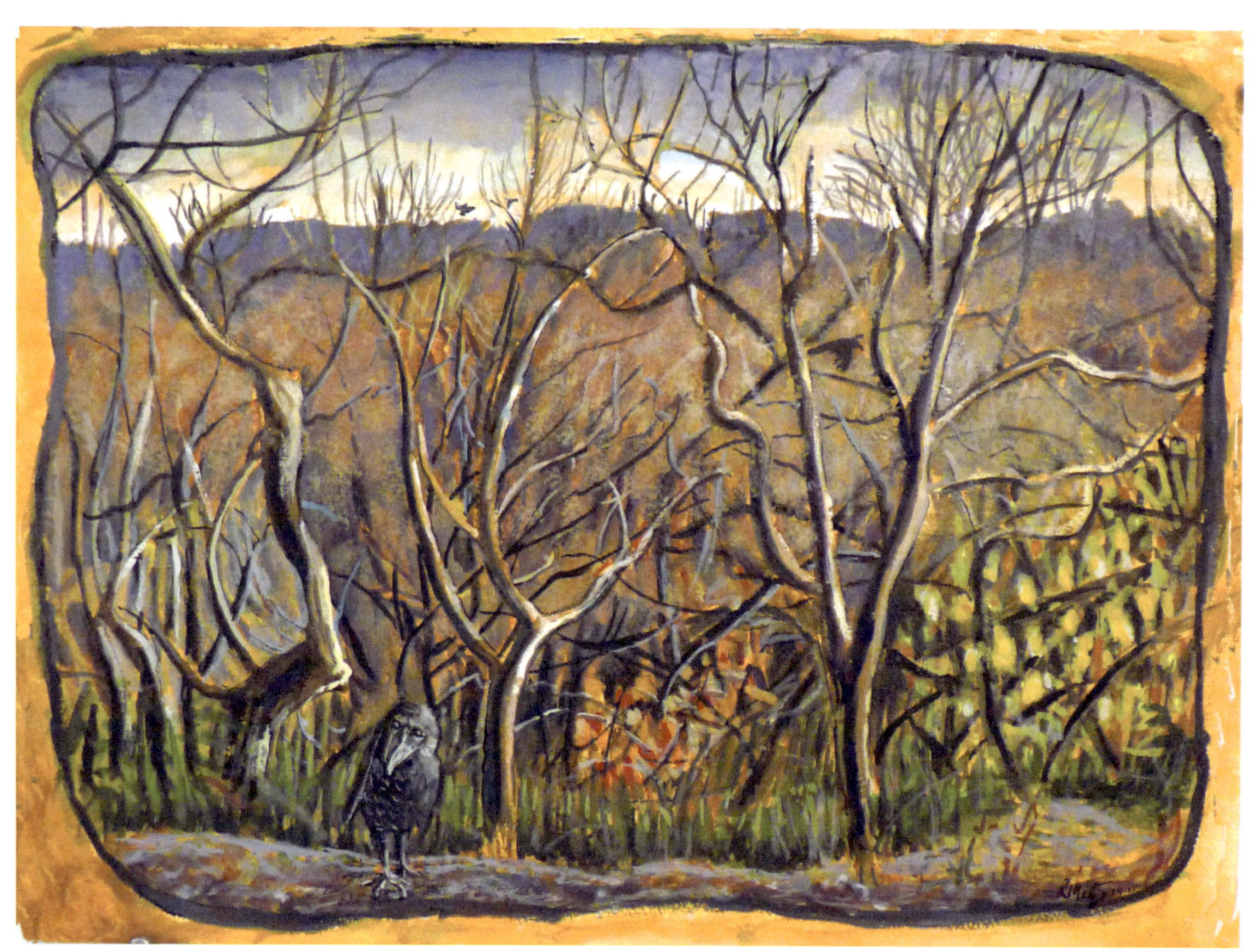

The Yellow Overlook

Walking through the oven-baked days,
looking far and long down the overlook,
I came upon a black bird
just standing there dark as day

Then I saw another flying past
Or was that a branch?
Far away near the horizon,
two—no three—more
bouncing just below the clouds

Now black bird is standing,
just five feet away
looking directly at me,
following my movements
with his ice-glaring eyes
But he—or she—says nothing,
quite content to afford me a glance

Then his head moves around like he's pointing
Squawk, Caw, Squawk
Is he really saying
"All of this—is for *all* of us?"
I give him a quizzical look

But he bobs his head several times
then raises his dark wings
and takes off for the gracious sky

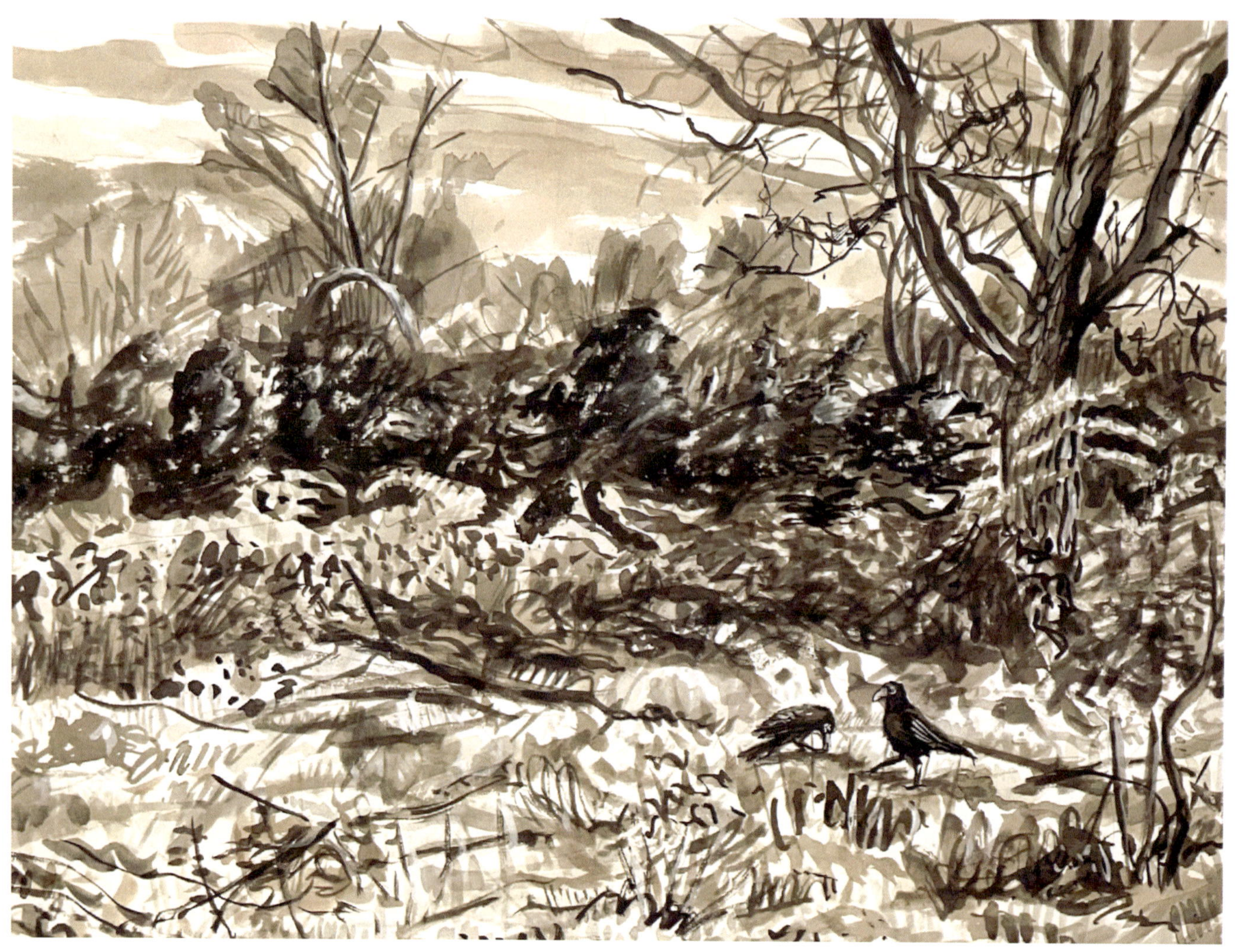

Rhythmic Meadow

Feels like the moonlight
It's not evening yet
breaking out in the day

We went out walking
The clouds still brooding
through the grass and the trees
The trees are raging
stubby grounds, and branches—
and the tall grasses wild
strewn still flying around
and impenetrable
The blue stems arise and
Everything is moving
brush against my leg
closer-closer, there see?

To tell time
Make for the tree line
follow the streams of clouds
where I'll be able to see
passing by
Soon—
all *the feathered beings*
Don't question the branches—
settle in for the evening
follow them and we'll see
in the limbs high above,
how to land in the moonlight
coming back to the roost

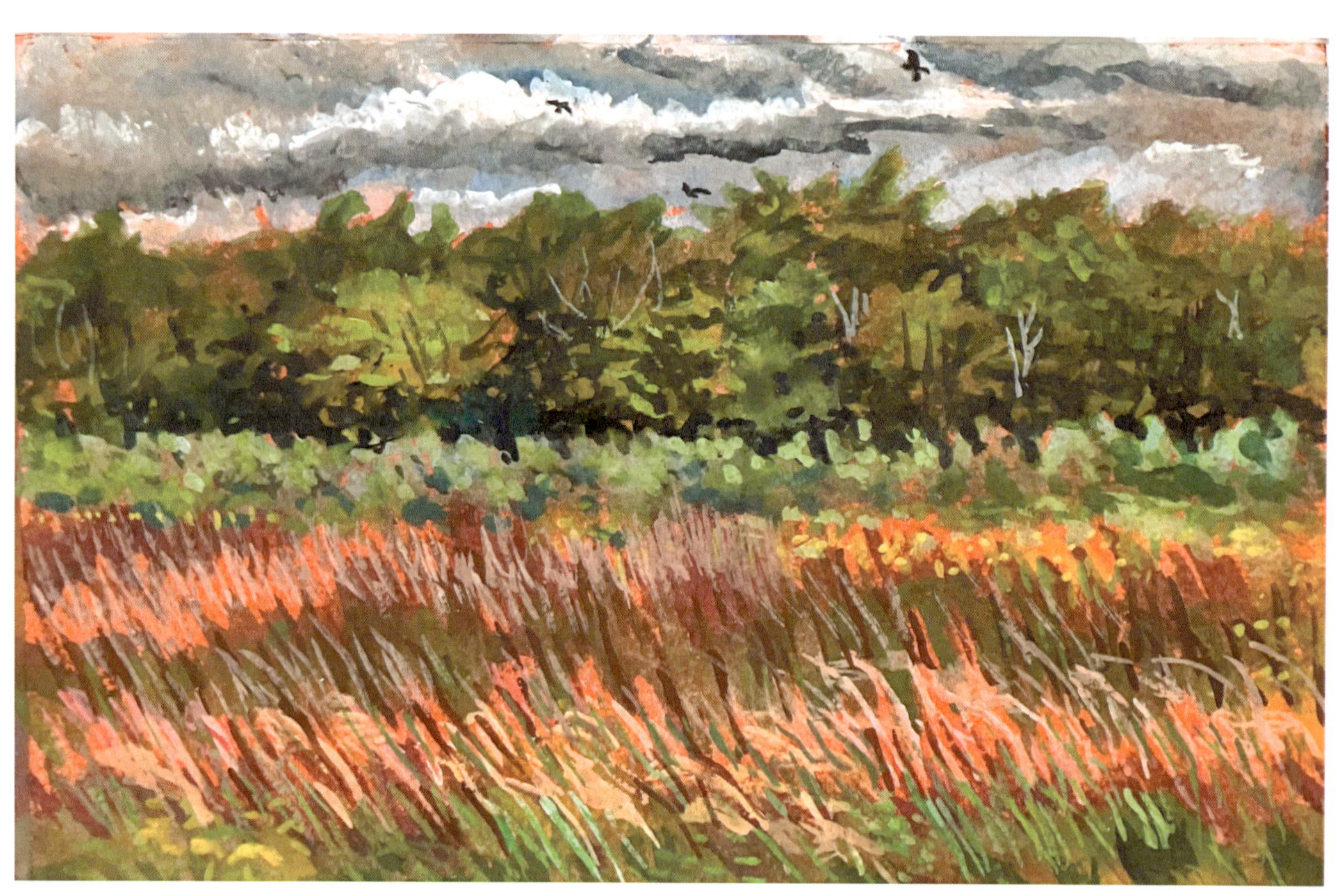

Roiling Red Meadow

The northern cold descends
evicting summer breezes
Agile autumn drunk with color
as leaves dance on their branches

The October red grasses
writhing like tentacles,
bend shuddering
without a will of their own

We can't stay still, clouds carry us afar
We've had our fill
darkened skies bode ill—
an atmospheric low
is descending.
Quickly let's fly
over the roiling live meadow
to the evergreen roost our home

A change is coming
to our days and nights,
coming to blow our mad world around
and who knows
where you will land
and where all of it went

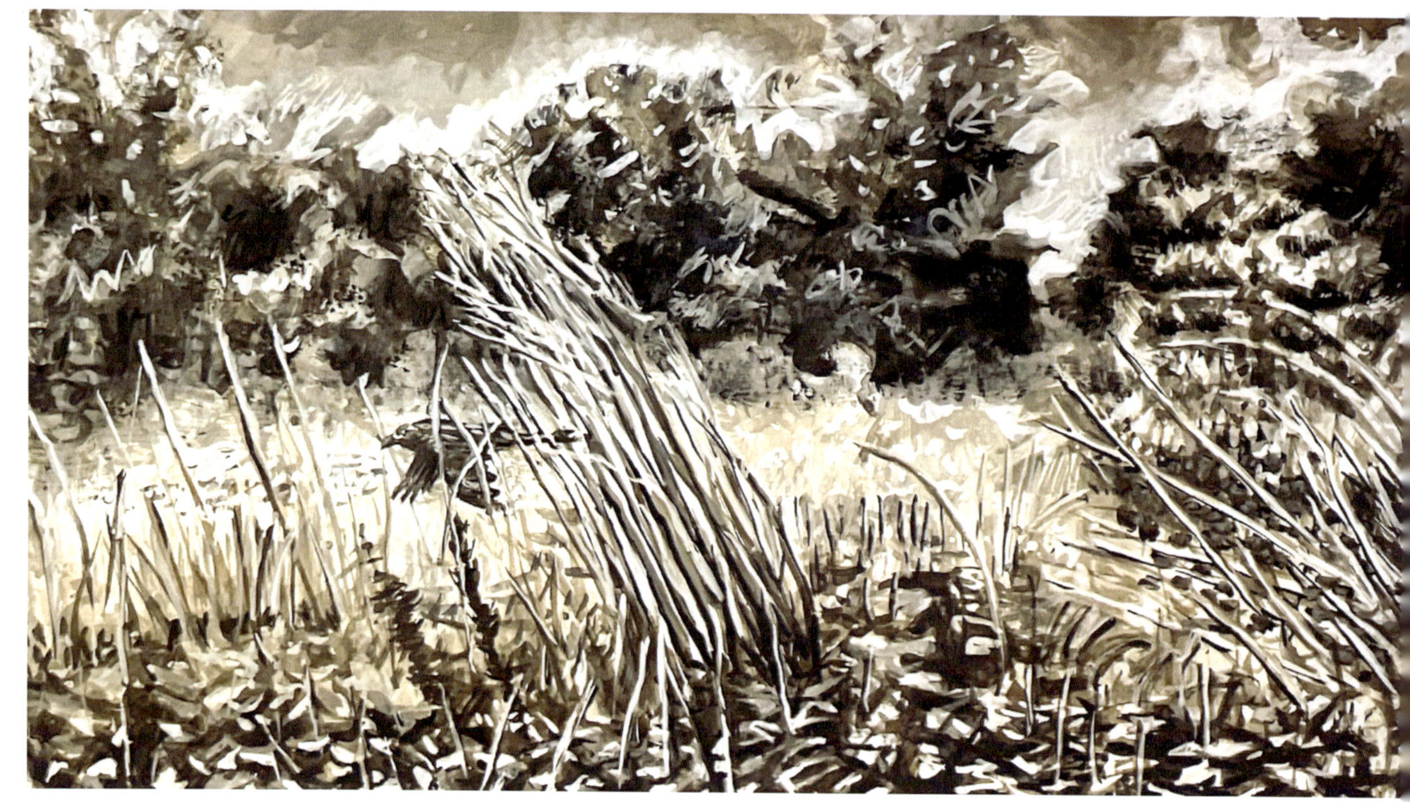

Coming To and Leaving the Meadow

Leaping large
I've come to the meadow
becoming the meadow
The tall stems—my hair
Gesticulating branches
loose limbed arms
Rich loamy soil
are skin, bones
and the roots

my red beating heart
Below in the bedrock—
legs to support me

Now a storm blows the grasses
bending in arcs
tossing and thrown,
Leaves rustle and blow
Now low
the black crow

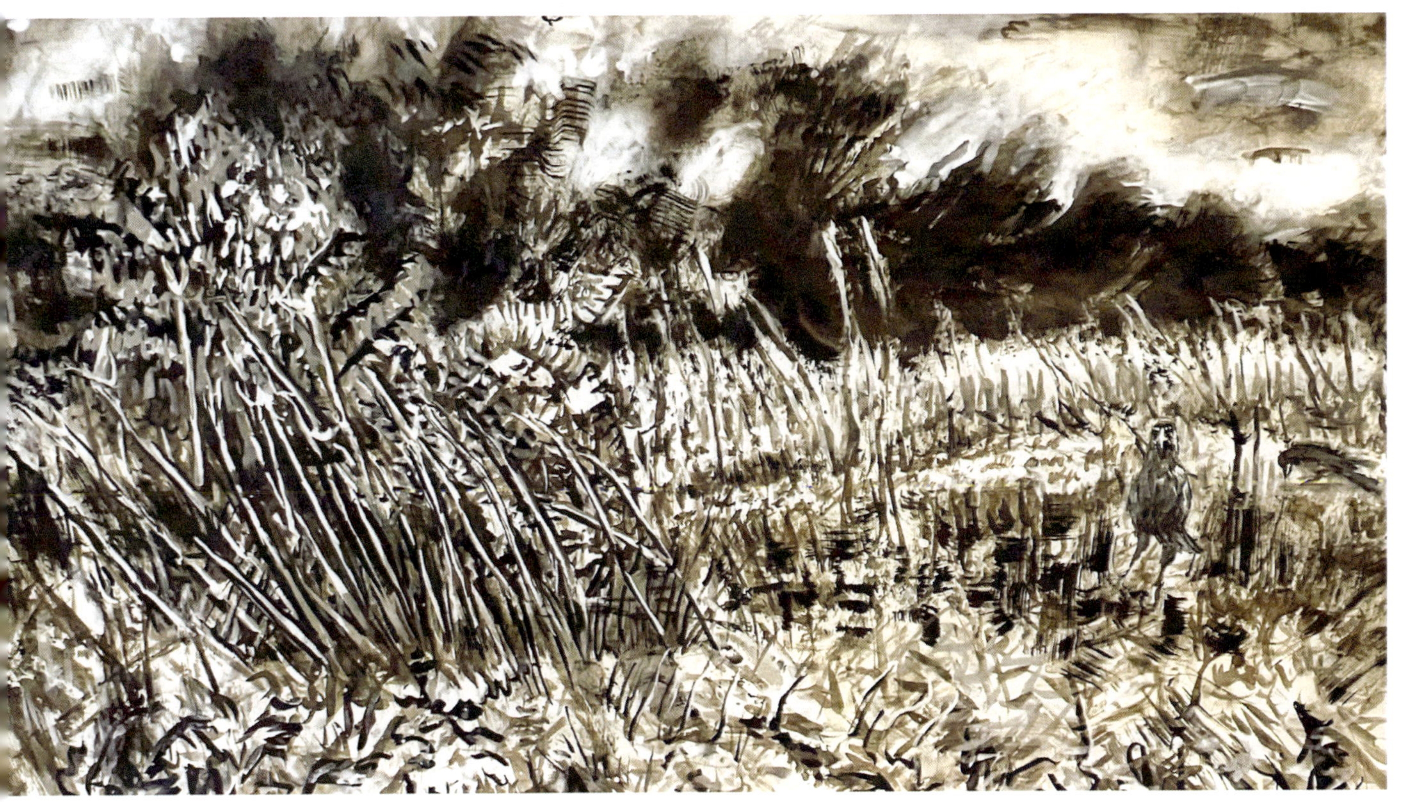

threading the stalks and shrubs
looking for mice and grubs.
Above in the whipping trees
autumn's menace knocks summer
and the branches and needles
sound like cabins thrown about
in great swirling clouds

I think I'll stay here
with the crows when I die
to chortle and mingle—
maybe I'll finally
learn how to live

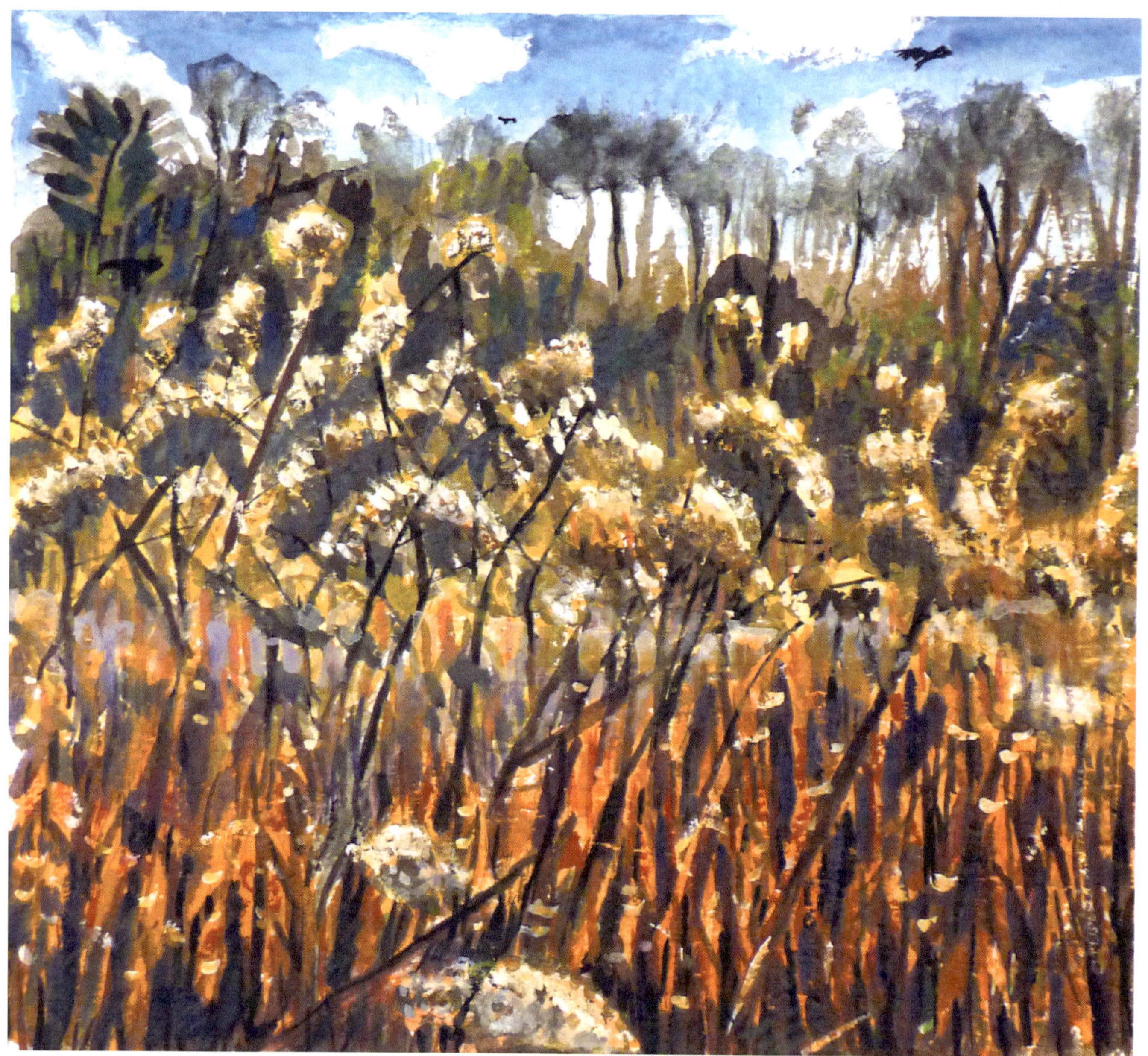

About the Author

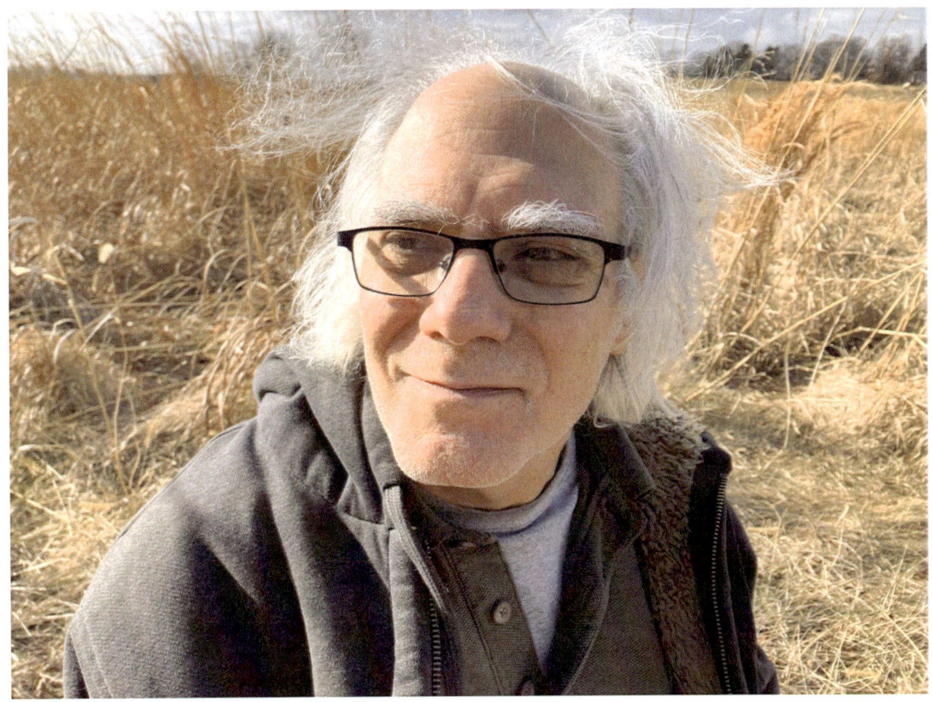

Richard Metz lives with his wife in northwest Philadelphia, not too far from where he grew up. His two grown sons live in the Philadelphia area. He attended Tyler School of Art, and earned an MFA from Maine College of Art. He retired from teaching high school art in 2019, and now focuses on nature, art, music, writing, environmental organizing, and spending time with family and friends. This is the author's second book of poems and paintings. His first one, published in 2025, was titled *A Murder of Crow*s.

www.mistermetz.com

www.ingramcontent.com/pod-product-compliance
Lightning Source LLC
Chambersburg PA
CBRC091246050726
47599CB00010B/1006